Multifamily Mastery
A GUIDE TO STRATEGIC PROPERTY OPTIMIZATION

By Dr. Tyler Billings

outskirts press

Multifamily Mastery
A Guide To Strategic Property Optimization
All Rights Reserved.
Copyright © 2024 Dr. Tyler Billings
v1.0

The opinions expressed in this manuscript are solely the opinions of the author and do not represent the opinions or thoughts of the publisher. The author has represented and warranted full ownership and/or legal right to publish all the materials in this book.

This book may not be reproduced, transmitted, or stored in whole or in part by any means, including graphic, electronic, or mechanical without the express written consent of the publisher except in the case of brief quotations embodied in critical articles and reviews.

Outskirts Press, Inc.
http://www.outskirtspress.com

ISBN: 978-1-9772-7159-4

Cover Photo © 2024 Dr. Tyler Billings. All rights reserved - used with permission.

Outskirts Press and the "OP" logo are trademarks belonging to Outskirts Press, Inc.

PRINTED IN THE UNITED STATES OF AMERICA

Introduction

Step into the dynamic world of multifamily property management with "Multifamily Mastery: A Guide to Strategic Property Optimization." This isn't just a book; it's a gateway to mastering the complexities and seizing the myriad opportunities in property management. Tailored for the discerning property manager, the astute real estate expert, and the forward-thinking investor — often referred to as multifamily operators — this book acts as your navigational tool. It empowers you not just to adapt but to thrive in the constantly evolving world of property management. Join us on this transformative expedition.

The multifamily property sector is dynamic, challenging, and rewarding. It requires a multifaceted approach that balances financial acumen, strategic planning, and a deep understanding of resident needs and market trends. In this book, we aim to equip you with a blend of time-tested techniques and cutting-edge strategies that will empower you to optimize every aspect of your property management practice.

From adopting dynamic pricing models that respond to market fluctuations to enhancing your property's online presence, from introducing value-added services to implementing cost-effective unit upgrades, and from fostering energy efficiency to building a strong community through resident retention programs – this book covers a wide spectrum of essential topics. Each chapter delves into a specific area of property management, offering practical insights, actionable strategies, and real-world examples.

Our journey together will be more than just a learning experience; it's an invitation to rethink traditional methods, embrace innovation, and visualize the future of property management. Whether you're managing a sprawling apartment community or a boutique residential building, the strategies outlined in this book are designed to help you elevate your property's appeal, maximize revenue, and create an environment where residents feel genuinely at home.

As you turn these pages, we encourage you to think critically, question conventional wisdom, and be open to new ideas. The field of property management is constantly evolving, and staying ahead requires both agility and foresight. With this guide, you are poised to not just meet the challenges of today but to seize the opportunities of tomorrow.

Let's embark on this journey of transformation and growth together. Here's to building thriving communities and successful property management ventures that stand the test of time!

Table of Contents

Introduction i

Chapter 1: Adopting a Dynamic Pricing Method.................. 1
    Understanding Market Trends and Setting Flexible Rent Prices... 1
    Adopting Demand-Responsive and Variable
        Lease Duration Pricing 3
    Tools and Software for Rent Price Optimization 5
    Market Analysis Template for Operators......................... 6

Chapter 2: Enhancing Online Visibility 10
    Crafting a Digital Identity: Websites and Social Media 10
    Sculpting an Engaging Website: 11
    Leveraging Social Media:...................................... 12
    Strategies for Virtual Tours and Digital Marketing.............. 13

Chapter 3: Introducing Value-Added Services 16
    Identifying and Implementing Additional Services for Revenue. 16
    Case Studies: Real-world Applications of Value-Added Services . 18

Chapter 4: Cost-Effective Unit Upgrades 20
    Selecting Upgrades That Attract Residents and
        Justify Higher Rents 20
    ROI Analysis on Various Upgrade Options 21

Chapter 5: Energy Efficiency for Cost Savings 25
  Implementing Energy-Saving Practices and Appliances 25
  Impact of Energy Efficiency on Operating Costs and
      Resident Appeal 28

Chapter 6: Implementing Pet-Friendly Policies 32
  Navigating the Benefits and Challenges of Pet-Friendly
      Environments 34

Chapter 7: Optimizing Unused Space 40
  Creative Ways to Transform Unused Spaces into
      Revenue Sources 40
  Increasing Revenue Potential through Space Optimization 43

Chapter 8: Marketing Strategies to Minimize Vacancies 46
  Effective Marketing Techniques to Keep Occupancy
      Rates High 46
  Leveraging Local Market Data for Targeted Advertising 49

Chapter 9: Developing Resident Retention Programs 52
  Building Community and Loyalty Through
      Retention Strategies....................................... 52
  Techniques for Reducing Turnover and Maintaining
      Long-Term Residents 54

Chapter 10: Conducting Regular Market Analysis 58
  Keeping Up with Market Changes and Competitive Pricing 58
  Tools and Methods for Ongoing Market Research 60

**Summary: Key Strategies for Optimizing Multifamily
  Property Management**.. 63

1
Adopting a Dynamic Pricing Method

*I*n the ever-evolving world of multifamily property management, the mastery of dynamic pricing models has become a critical key to unlocking revenue optimization. This chapter serves as your comprehensive guide, illuminating how you can adeptly adjust rent prices in response to the nuanced shifts of market demand and conditions. It's a journey that transcends mere competitiveness and profitability, venturing into the strategic realm of market trend analysis, flexible rent pricing, and effective use of rent optimization tools.

Understanding Market Trends and Setting Flexible Rent Prices

Embarking on the path of dynamic pricing begins with a deep dive into market research. Imagine pouring over data from various online rental platforms like Zillow and Apartments.com, local real estate reports, and industry publications. Here, you're not just collecting numbers; you're gathering stories of the market - stories told through data points like average rent prices, current vacancy rates, and the specific demographics of residents in your area.

For instance, a property manager noticing a surge in young professionals in their area might shift focus to amenities that appeal to this demographic, such as high-speed internet or a modern fitness center. Such targeted enhancements can justify higher rents, directly boosting revenue.

The art of comparative analysis involves looking at this data over time, like a historian studying the past to predict the future. You'll identify trends and shifts in the local rental market, helping shape your pricing strategy. For example, if year-over-year analysis shows an increasing demand for pet-friendly units, you might consider implementing pet-friendly policies, thus attracting a wider resident base and potentially commanding higher rents.

Seasonal variations in rental demand are akin to the changing seasons of nature. Each season brings its unique pattern, requiring tailored strategies. In university towns, for instance, demand might peak during the academic year start and ebb during the summer. By understanding these patterns, you can adjust your rental prices and marketing efforts accordingly, ensuring steady occupancy and optimized revenue throughout the year.

Regular competitor monitoring keeps you abreast of the market's pulse. By benchmarking against nearby properties, you gain insights into competitive rent prices, occupancy rates, and amenity offerings. This knowledge guides your decision-making, helping you stay competitive and desirable in the eyes of potential Residents. For example, if competitors are offering rent discounts during the off-season, you might consider similar or more attractive offers to maintain high occupancy rates.

Adopting Demand-Responsive and Variable Lease Duration Pricing

Embracing dynamic pricing in property management is similar to navigating a ship through ever-changing seas. This approach, marked by its agility and responsiveness, involves strategically adjusting rent prices in sync with the market's pulse. During high-demand periods, such as popular moving seasons or significant local events, rents are elevated to capitalize on the increased demand. Conversely, in slower market phases, reducing rent prices can maintain the property's allure, preventing vacancies and sustaining a steady stream of revenue.

The concept of dynamic pricing is not just about adjusting to the market's tempo; it's about maximizing every opportunity to optimize revenue. When the market is bustling, higher rents tap into the peak demand, capturing increased revenue potential. In quieter times, reduced rents act as a magnet for prospective residents, ensuring continuous occupancy and a stable income flow.

Variable lease duration pricing further refines your revenue strategy. This nuanced approach involves customizing rent prices based on the lease's term length, creating a balanced ecosystem of tenancy within your property. Short-term leases are priced at a premium, reflecting the higher costs and risks associated with frequent Resident turnovers. The premium pricing for short-term leases compensates for the inherent unpredictability and administrative efforts involved, ensuring that these leases contribute effectively to the property's revenue.

On the flip side, long-term leases, prized for their stability, might be offered at more attractive rates. This strategy isn't just about offering a discount; it's about fostering a sense of commitment and longevity among your prospective residents. By incentivizing longer lease terms with reduced rates or additional perks, such as complimentary amenities or services, property managers can cultivate a stable resident base. This stability is key to reducing frequent turnovers, which are often costly in terms of both marketing efforts and property maintenance. With longer leases, the property enjoys sustained occupancy, reducing the financial drain and operational burdens of frequent resident replacements.

This dual approach of demand-responsive and variable lease duration pricing creates a dynamic pricing environment where the property is always aligned with market conditions and prospective resident preferences. This alignment is crucial for optimizing revenue. By navigating these two aspects adeptly, property managers can ensure their properties are not only financially robust but also appealing and adaptive to the needs of the market.

In summary, adopting dynamic and variable lease duration pricing is a testament to a property manager's strategic foresight and adaptability. It's a proactive stance in revenue management, ensuring that every aspect of pricing is tuned to market dynamics and Resident behavior, ultimately leading to optimized revenue and a thriving property.

Tools and Software for Rent Price Optimization

In the field of rent pricing optimization, technology plays a crucial role. There are a variety of sophisticated software solutions available, such as YieldStar, LRO, RentMaximizer, and Revvy. These tools employ advanced algorithms and leverage extensive market data to help you make well-informed pricing decisions. By analyzing large sets of market data, they provide pricing recommendations that are in sync with the current market dynamics.

Additionally, comprehensive market analytics platforms like CoStar, Axiometrics, or ApartmentIQ are instrumental in offering in-depth insights into the latest market trends. This information is invaluable for setting rent prices that are both competitive and profitable. For example, such platforms might identify a growing number of remote workers moving into your area. This insight could lead you to enhance and promote co-working spaces within your property, appealing to this expanding demographic and potentially increasing your revenue.

Furthermore, integrating advanced pricing tools with your existing property management systems, such as Entrata, Yardi, OneSite, Rent Manager, or Appfolio, can greatly enhance the efficiency of your property management operations. This seamless integration does more than just ease your day-to-day tasks; it also ensures the effective execution of your pricing strategies. By doing so, it contributes significantly to the financial stability and growth of your property, ensuring that operational efficiency and strategic pricing go hand in hand for optimal financial performance.

By mastering these advanced pricing strategies and utilizing the appropriate technological tools, you, as a multifamily operator, can navigate the complexities of the rental market with increased confidence and accuracy. This chapter is designed to equip you with the necessary knowledge and skills to maximize your revenue potential while adapting to the ever-evolving demands of the rental market.

Market Analysis Template for Operators

To support thorough and effective market analysis, here is a foundational template designed for operators, providing a structured approach to identify key factors:

1. Property Name:
2. Date of Analysis:
3. Location/Area:

Market Data:
1. Average Area Rent:
2. Local Vacancy Rate:
3. Demographic Trends:
4. Seasonal Demand Fluctuations:

Competitor Analysis:
1. Competitor 1:
   - Rent Range:
   - Amenities:
   - Occupancy Rate:
   - Lease Terms:
2. Competitor 2:
   - [Include similar details]
3. Competitor 3:
   - [Include similar details]

Your Property Analysis:
- Current Rent Price:
- Amenities Offered:
- Current Occupancy Rate:
- Lease Terms:

Action Plan:
1. Suggested Rent Adjustments:

2. Potential Promotional Activities:
3. Projected Review Date for Adjustments:

Practical Examples and Applications

1. Scenario-Based Rent Adjustments: If market data shows increased demand during the summer, multifamily operators can plan rent hikes accordingly. Conversely, during winter, if demand drops, they can consider special promotions to attract Residents.
2. Strategic Promotions: Based on market analysis, during off-peak seasons, introducing incentives such as discounted rent for the first month or waived application fees can help maintain occupancy rates.
3. Adapting Lease Terms: Adjust lease pricing based on competitor analysis and demand forecasts. For example, offering lower rates for longer leases to ensure occupancy stability.
4. Regular Market Reviews: Establish a routine for revisiting and revising rent prices, based on the latest market data and competitor movements.

Conclusion

Dynamic pricing models are integral to modern property management, enabling multifamily operators to align their pricing strategies with real-time market conditions. The market analysis template provided serves as a blueprint for understanding market dynamics and making informed pricing decisions. By adopting these strategies, multifamily operators can enhance their property's revenue potential, ensuring both competitiveness and profitability.

Engaging Question for the Reader:

How can dynamic pricing models not only maximize your revenue potential but also adapt to changing market conditions and Resident expectations, ensuring that your property remains both competitive and fair in its pricing strategy?

Next, we will explore the importance of enhancing online visibility in Chapter 2, a crucial factor for attracting and retaining Residents in the digital age.

2

Enhancing Online Visibility

The digital landscape has become a pivotal arena for property management, especially in promoting multifamily properties. This chapter focuses on maximizing a property's online presence through innovative strategies in website development, social media engagement, virtual tours, and digital marketing. For each area, we will provide a detailed explanation of the technique, followed by actionable steps and real-world examples for implementation.

Crafting a Digital Identity: Websites and Social Media

In the digital era, the first impression of your multifamily property is often made online, long before a potential resident steps through your doors. This section of our guide, "Crafting a Digital Identity: Websites and Social Media," is dedicated to helping you create a compelling and effective online presence for your property. Here, we delve into the essential elements of developing a dynamic website and establishing a vibrant social media persona.

We understand that a website is more than just a digital brochure; it's the virtual front door to your property, a platform that should capture the essence of your community and invite engagement. Similarly, social media is not just about posting updates; it's a powerful tool for building relationships, fostering community, and enhancing your property's visibility in the digital landscape.

Through this section, we will guide you through the nuances of website design that resonates with your target audience, effective content strategies for social media, and how to integrate these digital assets into a cohesive online identity. You'll learn to navigate the digital realm with confidence, ensuring that your online presence not only attracts potential residents but also delights and engages your existing community. Welcome to the journey of transforming your property's digital footprint into a beacon of engagement and attraction.

Sculpting an Engaging Website:

Imagine a website that's not just visually appealing but is an oasis of user-friendliness. It's the digital front door to your property, and its design can significantly influence potential residents' perceptions. A website that loads quickly, is easy to navigate, and adapts flawlessly to different devices, particularly smartphones, is key to capturing the attention of modern residents.

Actionable Insight: Conduct an in-depth audit of your existing website. Evaluate its performance across various devices, assess its loading speed, and analyze the intuitiveness of its navigation.

Real-World Application: Consider a scenario where you revamp your website, introducing a layout that's both sleek and intuitive. Streamline the navigation menu and optimize images to ensure quick loading, thereby enhancing the overall user experience.

Leveraging Social Media:

In today's interconnected world, social media is the heartbeat of online engagement. It's about creating a vibrant community around your property. Regularly post content that resonates with your audience, be it updates about your property, highlights from community events, or valuable tips for residents. This isn't just about posts and likes; it's about fostering a sense of belonging and lifestyle around your property.

Actionable Insight: Develop a strategic social media plan with a consistent posting schedule. Focus on content that uniquely represents your property's character.

Real-World Application: Imagine launching a "Resident Tuesdays" feature on Instagram, where you spotlight different residents' stories or experiences each week, accompanied by captivating visuals of life at your property.

Strategies for Virtual Tours and Digital Marketing

As the real estate industry evolves, so does the need for multifamily operators to adopt and excel in these digital strategies.

We begin by exploring the world of virtual tours, a groundbreaking tool in today's property market. You'll learn how to create immersive, engaging virtual experiences that allow potential residents to explore and connect with your property from anywhere in the world. This section is designed to guide you through the process of conceptualizing, creating, and sharing high-quality virtual tours that captivate and intrigue your audience.

Moving beyond virtual tours, we then shift our focus to the expansive domain of digital marketing. Here, you'll be introduced to a range of digital marketing strategies tailored for the multifamily property market. From crafting compelling email campaigns to leveraging social media platforms and maximizing the potential of online rental listings, this section is filled with actionable insights and techniques. We will discuss how to effectively use digital tools to reach and engage your target audience, enhance your property's online visibility, and ultimately drive occupancy rates.

Whether you are a novice in the digital space or looking to refine your existing strategies, this section is designed to provide you with the knowledge and tools necessary to navigate the digital marketing landscape confidently. Get ready to embrace the digital revolution in property management and unlock new potential for your property.

Bringing Properties to Life with Virtual Tours:

Virtual tours are more than just a trendy tool; they're a window for potential residents to peek into their future homes. Especially in a world where remote interactions are becoming the norm, offering high-quality, 360-degree virtual tours can significantly enhance your property's appeal.

Actionable Insight: Collaborate with professionals to create detailed, immersive virtual tours of your property.

Real-World Application: Imagine embedding these interactive tours on your website and sharing them across your social media channels, inviting prospective residents to explore your property from the comfort of their homes.

Digital Marketing Techniques:

Digital marketing is an orchestra of various strategies, each playing a vital role in promoting your property. It's about harnessing the power of email campaigns, ensuring your property's presence on key online rental platforms, creating engaging content, and utilizing analytics to fine-tune your strategies.

Actionable Insight: Initiate an email marketing campaign,

regularly sending out newsletters that keep potential and current residents informed and engaged.

Real-World Application: Design a monthly newsletter that includes community updates, special offers, and property news. Encourage your residents to share their experiences and reviews online, and make sure to engage with their feedback professionally.

Conclusion

Enhancing online visibility is a dynamic and continuous process. It involves creating an engaging digital experience through your website, maintaining an active and interactive presence on social media, offering immersive virtual tours, and employing strategic digital marketing. By adopting these practices, multifamily operators can effectively attract and engage with a broader audience, ultimately leading to increased Resident interest and retention.

Engaging Question for the Reader:

In what ways can enhancing your property's online presence transform the way potential Residents perceive your property, and how can this digital footprint influence their decision-making process in choosing their next home?

In the next chapter, we will delve into the integration of value-added services, exploring how these can further augment your property's appeal and contribute to revenue growth.

3

Introducing Value-Added Services

*I*n today's multifamily property market, offering value-added services can significantly enhance Resident satisfaction and open up new revenue streams. This chapter focuses on how multifamily operators can identify, implement, and successfully manage additional services that not only cater to the needs and preferences of Residents but also boost the property's revenue potential.

Identifying and Implementing Additional Services for Revenue

The process of introducing value-added services begins with understanding Resident needs and market demands. Services such as in-unit laundry, high-speed internet, pet amenities, or premium parking options can greatly increase the attractiveness of your property. The key is to identify services that are both desirable to your Residents and viable for your property.

Engagement Strategy:

1. **Resident Surveys:** Engage directly with your residents through surveys. This crucial step allows you to capture their preferences and priorities, which in turn shapes your decision-making process. What do they value the most? Your residents' responses will pave the way for your service enhancement strategy.
2. **Market Research:** Take a deep dive into the trends and offerings in the competitive landscape. What are other properties offering? This analysis is vital in identifying gaps in the market and opportunities for your property to stand out.
3. **Feasibility Analysis:** Assess the practical aspects of introducing new services. What are the costs involved? How will they be managed? Consider forming alliances with local businesses or service providers for effective and efficient implementation.

Real-Life Examples and Implementation:

- Picture a scenario where resident feedback highlights a demand for pet-friendly services. You could introduce a dedicated pet grooming area or collaborate with a local pet care provider, offering discounted services right at

their doorstep.
- For properties with a considerable number of remote workers, upgrading to high-speed internet and establishing a modern co-working space can fulfill a critical need, making your property an attractive option for this growing demographic.

Case Studies: Real-world Applications of Value-Added Services

1. Enhancing Security and Technology:
   - A residential community in an urban setting implemented a state-of-the-art security system, featuring keyless entry and 24/7 surveillance. This upgrade not only bolstered Resident safety but also appealed to the tech-savvy renter demographic. Through interactive sessions and demonstrations, multifamily operators ensure a smooth transition for residents, enhancing their sense of security and comfort.

2. Fostering Community Through Gardening
   - Another property introduced a community gardening program, offering residents individual plots for growing their own plants and vegetables. The multifamily operators organize regular workshops and social events around gardening, fostering community spirit and enhancing Resident satisfaction.

3. Prioritizing Wellness and Fitness
   - An apartment community integrated wellness programs by offering on-site fitness classes and health workshops. The multifamily operators engage Residents by involving them in the scheduling process, ensuring the programs were tailored to their preferences and availability.

Conclusion

Integrating value-added services is a strategic approach to not just enhance the living experience of your residents but also to open up new avenues for revenue generation. Through thoughtful planning, engaging with residents, and strategic implementation, you can transform your property into a more desirable and financially thriving community.

Engaging Question for the Reader:

As you contemplate the future of your property, ask yourself: What unique value-added services could you introduce that would not only elevate the living experience of your residents but also set your property apart in a competitive market?

In our next chapter, we explore the realm of cost-effective unit upgrades, revealing how they can further enhance the appeal and value of your property.

4
Cost-Effective Unit Upgrades

*I*n the multifamily property industry, unit upgrades are a strategic way to enhance the appeal of a property and justify higher rents. This chapter focuses on identifying which upgrades are most effective in attracting Residents and providing a significant return on investment (ROI). It includes a detailed discussion on how to select upgrades, perform ROI analysis, and provides a practical ROI table template for multifamily operators to use in their evaluation process.

Selecting Upgrades That Attract Residents and Justify Higher Rents

The process of selecting upgrades involves balancing Resident desires with cost-effective investments that add real value to the property. Key areas often ripe for upgrades include kitchens and bathrooms, technological enhancements, and features that improve the overall livability and energy efficiency of a unit.

Engagement Strategy:

- **Resident Surveys and Feedback:** Engage with your Residents through surveys or feedback sessions to understand their needs and desires. This direct input can guide you in prioritizing upgrades that will have the most impact.
- **Market Analysis**: Examine local rental market trends to identify which features are most sought after by Residents. This might include trends like smart home technology, eco-friendly appliances, or modern design aesthetics.
- **Cost-Benefit Analysis:** Evaluate each potential upgrade for its cost versus the potential increase in rental value. Consider both the immediate cost and the long-term benefits in terms of property value and Resident satisfaction.

Examples of Implementation:

- Upgrading kitchens with new countertops, efficient appliances, and modern cabinetry.
- Installing smart home devices like programmable thermostats and smart locks, which are increasingly popular and can offer convenience and security to Residents.

ROI Analysis on Various Upgrade Options

Performing an ROI analysis is crucial to understanding the financial implications of each upgrade. This involves calculating the cost of the upgrade against the potential increase in rental income, and how long it will take for this increased income to cover the upgrade costs.

ROI Table Template:

Upgrade Option	Cost of Upgrade ($)	Additional Monthly Rent ($)	Break-Even Point (Months) Cost/ Monthly Rent	Notes
Kitchen Renovation				Include specific elements like appliances, countertops
Bathroom Renovation				Detail changes like new fixtures, tiling
Smart Home Features				List features like thermostats, locks
Energy-Efficient Appliances				Specify types, e.g., ENERGY STAR rated

Instructions for Use:

1. **Detailed Upgrade Costs:** Enter the full estimated cost for each upgrade.
2. **Estimate Rent Increase:** Determine the potential increase in monthly rent each upgrade can command.

3. **Calculate Break-Even Point:** Divide the total cost by the additional monthly rent to find out how many months it will take to recover the investment.

Case Studies on Successful Upgrades

1. **Comprehensive Kitchen and Bathroom Remodels:** A property executed full-scale renovations of kitchens and bathrooms, including high-end fixtures and finishes. This led to a substantial increase in rent and attracted a more affluent Resident demographic, with the investment recouped in approximately 24 months.
2. **Smart Home Technology Implementation:** Another property incorporated smart home technologies, catering to a tech-savvy renter base. These upgrades, while relatively low in cost, resulted in a swift ROI due to their popularity and the ability to slightly increase rents.

Conclusion

Strategically chosen unit upgrades can significantly enhance the attractiveness and profitability of a multifamily property. By engaging with Residents to understand their needs, analyzing the market for trends, and conducting thorough ROI analyses, multifamily operators can make informed decisions that benefit both the property and its residents.

Engaging Question for the Reader:

Reflect on how strategic, cost-effective unit upgrades could impact Resident retention and satisfaction. What specific upgrades would most significantly increase the perceived value and desirability of your units?

In the next chapter, we will explore the adoption of energy-efficient practices, highlighting their importance in reducing operational costs and their growing appeal among environmentally conscious Residents.

5
Energy Efficiency for Cost Savings

Energy efficiency is increasingly vital in multifamily property management, not just for its environmental benefits but also for its substantial impact on reducing operating costs and enhancing Resident appeal. This chapter is dedicated to exploring the implementation of energy-saving practices and appliances and analyzing how these initiatives can positively impact both operating costs and Resident satisfaction. It provides detailed strategies and actionable items for multifamily operators aiming to make their properties more energy-efficient and appealing to a modern, eco-conscious Resident base.

Implementing Energy-Saving Practices and Appliances

The shift towards energy-efficient operations in multifamily property management is more than just a trend; it's a holistic approach that significantly impacts both the environment and the property's bottom line. Implementing energy-saving practices and appliances requires a multifaceted strategy, integrating both advanced technology and sustainable operational practices across the property.

This transition to energy efficiency is not just about installing a few energy-saving devices; it involves rethinking and redesigning the property's energy usage from the ground up. It starts with an assessment of current energy consumption and identifying areas where improvements can be made. This could include everything from the lighting systems to HVAC units, from water heaters to appliances in common areas and individual units.

Actionable Steps for Energy Efficiency:

1. **Comprehensive Energy Audit:** Partner with energy efficiency experts to conduct a thorough audit of the property. This audit should identify all potential areas for energy savings, from appliances to insulation.
2. **Energy-Efficient Appliance Upgrades:** Systematically replace older appliances with ENERGY STAR-rated models. Focus on appliances that consume the most energy, like refrigerators, water heaters, and HVAC systems.
3. **Transition to LED Lighting:** Replace all existing lighting with LED alternatives, which offer longer life spans and lower energy consumption. Consider sensor-based

lighting systems in common areas to further reduce energy waste.
4. **Enhancing Insulation and Sealing:** Invest in better insulation materials and sealant solutions to minimize energy loss, especially in older buildings. Pay particular attention to roofs, windows, and doorways.
5. **Smart Thermostat Installation:** Implement programmable or smart thermostats that allow for more efficient heating and cooling management, reducing unnecessary energy use.

Engaging Residents in Energy-Saving Practices:

- **Energy Conservation Workshops:** Host workshops or webinars to educate Residents on the importance of energy conservation and how they can contribute.
- **Incentive Programs for Energy Reduction:** Develop incentive programs that reward Residents for reducing their energy consumption. This could include competitions or rewards for the most energy-efficient units.
- **Regular Updates and Communication:** Keep Residents informed about the property's energy-saving initiatives and progress. This could be through newsletters, community boards, or digital platforms.

Impact of Energy Efficiency on Operating Costs and Resident Appeal

The adoption of energy-saving measures in property management is a strategic move that yields dual benefits: it substantially lowers operating costs and enhances the property's appeal to both prospective and current residents. By integrating energy-efficient practices and technologies, properties can experience a marked reduction in energy consumption, leading to decreased utility expenses and a more cost-effective operation overall.

This shift towards energy efficiency is not only about installing energy-saving devices but also about cultivating a culture of sustainability within the property. From upgrading to high-efficiency appliances to retrofitting buildings with better insulation and energy-efficient windows, each step contributes to a significant reduction in energy usage. For example, replacing traditional lighting with LED fixtures, or installing programmable thermostats and low-flow water fixtures, can have a profound impact on reducing energy bills.

Moreover, these energy-saving measures often translate into an enhanced living experience for residents. Features such as improved insulation lead to more comfortable living conditions, maintaining a consistent indoor temperature and reducing noise pollution. Similarly, the use of energy-efficient appliances and lighting contributes to a modern, eco-friendly living environment, which is increasingly important to environmentally conscious residents.

Furthermore, properties that demonstrate a commitment to energy efficiency often gain a competitive edge in the market. Prospective residents who are environmentally aware or looking to reduce their own utility costs are more likely to be attracted to properties that prioritize sustainability. Current residents also appreciate the efforts to create a greener living space, which can lead to increased satisfaction and retention rates.

Incorporating energy-efficient practices also positions a property as a responsible and forward-thinking community leader. It reflects a commitment to reducing the property's carbon footprint and contributing positively to the wider environmental conversation, an aspect that resonates well with many residents today.

In essence, the implementation of energy-saving measures is a smart investment for multifamily operators. It not only results in tangible cost savings but also adds intrinsic value to the property, making it more desirable to residents who value sustainability and cost efficiency. This approach not only contributes to a healthier environment but also fosters a positive image and reputation for the property in the competitive real estate market.

Reducing Operating Costs:

- **Utility Cost Reduction:** Efficient appliances and systems lower the overall utility costs for the property. This is particularly significant in properties where utilities are included in the rental price.

- **Long-Term Savings:** Energy-efficient appliances and practices often lead to reduced maintenance needs and longer replacement cycles, translating to long-term cost savings.

Enhancing Resident Appeal:

- **Attracting a Broader Resident Base:** Eco-friendly features often decide for environmentally conscious Residents, widening the potential Resident base.
- **Improving Resident Retention:** Residents who perceive their landlords as environmentally responsible and concerned about decreasing utility costs are more likely to be satisfied and remain at the property longer.

Conclusion

Energy efficiency is a critical aspect of modern property management, offering benefits that extend beyond environmental stewardship. By adopting energy-efficient practices and appliances, multifamily operators not only contribute to a healthier planet but also realize significant savings in operating costs and increase the attractiveness of their properties to Residents. The strategies and actions outlined in this chapter provide a roadmap for multifamily operators to effectively implement and benefit from energy-efficient initiatives.

Engaging Question for the Reader:

How might the implementation of energy-efficient practices and appliances in your property serve as a catalyst for broader environmental responsibility, and what impact could this have on the perception of your brand in the eyes of current and prospective Residents?

In the next chapter, we will delve into the adoption of pet-friendly policies, exploring how they can broaden the Resident pool, enhance Resident satisfaction, and open up new avenues for revenue generation

6

Implementing Pet-Friendly Policies

In the contemporary rental landscape, the trend of pet-friendly policies is rapidly gaining momentum, emerging as a key factor in the decision-making process for a significant number of residents. Recognizing this shift, this chapter is dedicated to navigating multifamily operators through the multifaceted process of cultivating a pet-friendly environment. The creation of such a space is not just about allowing pets; it involves a thoughtful consideration of how this decision impacts the community as a whole, balancing the benefits with potential challenges.

This chapter delves into the numerous advantages of implementing pet-friendly policies. From enhancing the appeal of your property to a wider range of residents to fostering a more vibrant and inclusive community atmosphere, the presence of pets can significantly boost resident satisfaction and retention. We explore how properties that welcome pets often see increased interest and higher occupancy rates, as pet owners seek out accommodations that cater to their furry companions.

However, transitioning to a pet-friendly environment also presents its own set of challenges. Multifamily operators must navigate issues such as noise management, potential property damage, and ensuring the comfort and safety of all residents, including those without pets. This chapter provides comprehensive strategies for addressing these challenges, from establishing clear pet policies and behavior guidelines to designing pet-specific amenities and spaces within the property.

A crucial aspect of embracing pet-friendly practices is the structuring of pet fees and pet rent policies. This section offers detailed guidance on developing a fair and effective fee structure that compensates for potential additional maintenance and ensures responsible pet ownership. We discuss various models for pet fees and rents, weighing their pros and cons, and provide insights on how to integrate these fees into lease agreements in a way that is transparent and agreeable to pet owners.

In essence, this chapter serves as a guide for multifamily operators to navigate the growing trend of pet-friendly housing. By embracing these practices and addressing the accompanying challenges with well-thought-out strategies, multifamily operators can not only enhance the appeal of their properties but also contribute to the creation of a more dynamic and inclusive community for all residents.

Navigating the Benefits and Challenges of Pet-Friendly Environments

Establishing a pet-friendly environment within a property can be a transformative move, significantly enhancing its appeal to a broad spectrum of potential and current residents. This inclusivity towards pet owners can lead to improved occupancy rates and heightened resident satisfaction, as it caters to the growing number of pet owners who view their pets as cherished family members. The presence of pets often contributes to a more vibrant, community-oriented atmosphere, which can be a strong selling point for the property.

However, the decision to create a pet-friendly environment comes with its own set of challenges that require careful management and strategic planning. One of the primary concerns is addressing pet-related noise, which can potentially disrupt the peace and comfort of other residents. Effective solutions might include establishing designated 'quiet hours' or soundproofing certain areas to minimize noise transmission.

Another significant challenge is managing pet-related damage. Pets, while adorable, can sometimes cause wear and tear to the property, from scratched surfaces to accidents in common areas. To mitigate these risks, multifamily operators might consider implementing pet policies that include damage deposits or fees, providing resources for pet training, or designating specific pet-friendly zones within the property.

Additionally, maintaining the comfort and well-being of all residents, including those without pets, is crucial. This involves ensuring that common areas remain clean and hygienic, implementing rules regarding pet behavior and leash requirements, and possibly designating certain areas as pet-free zones to accommodate residents who may have allergies or phobias.

Creating a pet-friendly environment also opens up opportunities for community-building activities centered around pets, such as pet meet-and-greets or dog-walking groups, fostering a sense of camaraderie and social engagement among residents.

In summary, while transitioning to a pet-friendly property can boost its appeal and resident satisfaction, it requires a balanced approach that addresses potential challenges head-on. By implementing thoughtful policies and amenities geared towards both pet owners and those without pets, multifamily operators can create a harmonious living environment that appeals to a wider resident base, ultimately enhancing the property's desirability and community spirit.

Engagement Strategies for Pet-Friendly Policies:

1. **Conducting Resident Surveys:** Engage with both current and potential residents to gauge their interest in pet-friendly amenities and their concerns.
2. **Developing Comprehensive Pet Policies:** Create clear policies regarding types of allowed pets, breed or size

restrictions, and designated pet areas. This helps in managing expectations and maintaining harmony within the community.

3. **Incorporating Community Feedback:** Involve the Resident community in policy development to ensure buy-in and adherence.

Examples of Pet-Friendly Amenities and Services:

- Establishing pet walking or sitting services for busy pet owners.
- Hosting community events like pet meetups or educational sessions on pet care.

Challenges and Mitigation Strategies:

- Noise Management: Implement rules about noise control and provide guidelines for dealing with noisy pets.
- Dealing with Damage: Set clear guidelines for pet-related damage and their repercussions. Regular property inspections can help identify issues early.

Structuring Pet Fees and Pet Rent Policies

The implementation of pet fees and pet rent is a strategic and practical response to the unique challenges that come with pet-friendly policies. These financial measures are designed to balance the costs incurred by the property as a result of accommodating pets, which often includes increased wear and tear, more intensive maintenance requirements, and additional cleaning services. By introducing these fees, multifamily operators can ensure that the added expenses associated with maintaining a pet-friendly environment are equitably shared, thereby safeguarding the property's financial health and sustainability.

More than just a financial buffer, these pet-related fees also encourage responsible pet ownership among residents. They serve as a reminder of the accountability that comes with having a pet in a shared living space. Setting clear guidelines and fees for pet owners helps to maintain the quality and cleanliness of the property, ensuring that all residents, both with and without pets, can enjoy a comfortable and well-maintained living environment. In this way, pet fees and pet rent are not only about offsetting costs but also about promoting a harmonious community where the needs and comfort of all residents are respected and upheld.

Actionable Steps for Structuring Pet Fees:

1. **Competitive Analysis:** Research pet fees and pet rents in the local market to establish a competitive yet fair pricing structure.
2. **Transparent Fee Structure:** Clearly outline the specifics of pet fees and rents, explaining what these charges cover.
3. **Effective Policy Communication:** Ensure pet policies, including fee structures, are clearly communicated and

included in lease agreements. Provide this information during property tours and leasing discussions.

Examples of Pet Fee Structures:

- A non-refundable pet deposit to cover potential damage.
- A tiered pet rent system based on pet size or number of pets.

Benefits of Pet-Friendly Policies:

- **Attracting and Retaining Residents:** Pet-friendly policies can be a major draw for pet owners and can significantly reduce Resident turnover.
- Community Building: Pets often help in creating a sense of community among residents, leading to a more engaged and connected Resident base.

Promotional and Marketing Strategies:

- Marketing the Property as Pet-Friendly: Utilize marketing materials and online listings to highlight the property's pet-friendly amenities and policies.
- Collaborations and Partnerships: Consider partnering with local pet businesses or veterinarians for promotions or events, enhancing the appeal to pet owners.

Conclusion

Implementing pet-friendly policies can be a significant value-add for a property, attracting a wider pool of potential Residents and fostering a sense of community. By carefully balancing the benefits and challenges, and establishing clear, fair pet fee structures, multifamily operators can create a harmonious and attractive living environment for all residents, including those with furry friends.

Question for the reader:

As you consider the implementation of pet-friendly policies in your property management strategy, reflect on this: How can embracing a pet-friendly environment not only cater to the needs of pet-owning Residents but also shape the overall community culture and identity of your property? How might this approach influence both Resident satisfaction and your property's marketability?

In the next chapter, we will explore the transformation of unused spaces within the property, looking at how these areas can be repurposed into revenue-generating amenities or services

7

Optimizing Unused Space

One of the untapped opportunities in property management is the efficient utilization of unused space. This chapter focuses on transforming these spaces into functional areas that can significantly increase a property's revenue potential. We will explore various strategies for identifying and converting unused spaces, highlight successful case studies, and conclude with a thought-provoking question for multifamily operators to consider.

Creative Ways to Transform Unused Spaces into Revenue Sources

Transforming unused spaces within a property into valuable assets requires a well-thought-out strategic approach. This process isn't just about filling empty areas; it's about reimagining these spaces to develop amenities or services that resonate with residents' desires and lifestyles, while also providing financial benefits to the property. By identifying and creatively repurposing areas such as unused basements, rooftops, or common areas, multifamily operators can add significant value to their properties. These transformations have the potential to enhance the living experience for residents, making the property more attractive and competitive in the rental market.

For instance, converting an underutilized basement into a fitness center or a communal workspace can cater to the growing demand for health and work-life balance amenities. Similarly, transforming a rooftop into a garden or leisure space can offer residents a unique and appealing area to relax and socialize, greatly enhancing the appeal of the property. Each of these modifications not only improves the quality of life for residents but also opens up new revenue streams, such as rental fees for space usage or increased property value. This strategic approach to utilizing unused spaces is a proactive way to increase the property's marketability and profitability, ensuring that both residents and property owners benefit from these enhancements.

Strategies for Space Optimization:

1. **Identify Underutilized Areas:** Conduct a comprehensive analysis of the property to pinpoint spaces that are currently not being used to their full potential.
2. **Understand Resident Demands**: Engage with Residents to gauge their needs and interests. This helps in tailoring

the space to something that adds value to their living experience.

3. **Cost-Benefit Analysis:** Evaluate the investment required to transform these spaces against the potential revenue they could generate. This includes considering the costs of renovation, maintenance, and any additional staffing needs.

Ideas for Revenue-Generating Transformations:

- **Leased Retail Spaces:** Convert ground floor or street-facing spaces into areas that can be leased to retailers, cafes, or small businesses.
- **Rental Storage Units:** If storage is a premium, transforming basements or other unused areas into storage units can provide Residents with a much-needed service while generating rental income.
- **Specialized Amenities:** Amenities like a community kitchen, a small cinema room, or a workshop space can be rented out to Residents or external parties for events.

Case Studies on Successful Space Optimizations

1. Multifunctional Community Room
A residential community converted an unused lobby area into a multifunctional community room. Equipped with modular furniture, a kitchenette, and audio-visual equipment, the space could be rented out for private events,

classes, or meetings, creating a new revenue stream for the property.

2. Rooftop Lounge and Event Space
An urban apartment building transformed its neglected rooftop into a stylish lounge and event space. This area, complete with a bar, seating, and panoramic city views, became highly sought-after for events and gatherings, offering a significant boost in rental income.

3. On-Site Fitness Center
Another property turned an underused basement space into a fully-equipped fitness center. They offered memberships not only to residents but also to the public, creating a continuous revenue stream while enhancing the property's appeal.

Increasing Revenue Potential through Space Optimization

Optimizing unused spaces within a property goes beyond mere aesthetic enhancement and functional improvements; it unlocks new opportunities for revenue generation, serving as a catalyst for financial growth. By creatively transforming these underutilized areas, multifamily operators can unveil new rentable spaces that were previously overlooked, thereby maximizing the property's earning potential. This could involve converting a vacant rooftop into an exclusive event space, transforming an unused basement into a state-of-the-art gym, or turning an empty courtyard into a charming communal garden. Each of these revamped spaces not only adds value to the property but also becomes a potential source of additional income.

Moreover, these newly developed areas can provide premium amenities that elevate the property's market appeal, justifying higher rent prices. For instance, a well-designed rooftop lounge or a modern co-working space within the property can significantly enhance its desirability, attracting residents willing to pay more for these exclusive features. Additionally, these enhancements can broaden the resident base, appealing to a wider demographic looking for properties that offer more than just the basics. From young professionals seeking properties with convenient work-from-home spaces to pet owners looking for properties with dedicated pet areas, the right transformations can cater to a diverse range of preferences. Ultimately, this strategic use of space not only improves the living experience for current and future residents but also serves as a driving force in boosting the property's revenue potential, making it a more lucrative and competitive option in the housing market.

Conclusion

Effectively utilizing unused spaces presents a significant opportunity for multifamily operators to enhance both the Resident experience and the property's revenue potential. By creatively repurposing these areas, multifamily operators can add significant value to their properties, making them more competitive and attractive in the market.

Engaging Question for the Reader:

As you assess the unused spaces within your property, consider: What unique or underrepresented needs can these spaces fulfill for your Residents, and how can their transformation directly contribute to your property's financial growth and competitive edge?

Next, we will explore the necessity and benefits of conducting regular market analysis to stay informed and adaptive in the ever-changing landscape of property management.

8

Marketing Strategies to Minimize Vacancies

A critical aspect of successful property management is maintaining high occupancy rates. This chapter is designed to guide multifamily operators through effective marketing strategies aimed at minimizing vacancies and optimizing revenue. By leveraging local market data and employing targeted advertising techniques, multifamily operators can attract and retain residents more effectively.

Effective Marketing Techniques to Keep Occupancy Rates High

Maintaining high occupancy rates in multifamily property management hinges on a deep and nuanced understanding of your target audience. Knowing who your potential residents are – their needs, preferences, and lifestyle choices – is crucial for tailoring your marketing strategies effectively. It's about creating a connection between what your property offers and what your prospective residents are seeking.

To effectively engage with this audience, a diverse array of marketing techniques needs to be employed. This means not just casting a wide net, but also ensuring that the net is woven with precision to catch the right audience. For instance, if your property caters to young professionals, your marketing efforts might focus more on showcasing amenities like high-speed internet, modern co-working spaces, or proximity to urban nightlife and business districts. Conversely, if your property is more suited for families, highlighting aspects like safety, nearby schools, and family-friendly community events would be more effective.

Digital marketing plays a pivotal role in reaching potential residents. This includes having a strong online presence through a well-designed website, active social media engagement, and strategic online advertising. Utilizing search engine optimization (SEO) to improve your property's online visibility and targeting specific demographics through paid social media campaigns are essential tactics.

Moreover, offline marketing strategies, such as hosting open houses, community events, and collaborating with local businesses, can also significantly enhance visibility. These tactics not only draw attention to your property but also help build a sense of community that appeals to potential residents.

Beyond just attracting residents, your marketing efforts should also focus on creating an emotional connection. This involves telling a story about your property that resonates with your target audience, one that makes them envision themselves living and thriving in your community.

In essence, keeping occupancy rates high is a dynamic process that requires a blend of strategic marketing, deep audience understanding, and a keen sense of storytelling. By employing these techniques thoughtfully, you can effectively reach and resonate with potential residents, keeping your property vibrant and fully occupied.

Strategies for Effective Marketing:

1. **Understanding Your Target Market:** Conduct research to understand the demographics and preferences of your ideal residents. This insight will inform the tone and content of your marketing efforts.
2. **Utilizing Digital Platforms:** In today's digital age, online platforms are crucial for marketing. This includes maintaining an updated and engaging website, active social media presence, and listings on popular rental websites.
3. **Creative Content Creation:** Develop appealing content that showcases the unique features of your property. This could include virtual tours, Resident testimonials, and high-quality photographs.

4. **Community Engagement:** Host and promote community events to not only engage current Residents but also to attract potential Residents. This can create a sense of community and belonging which is appealing to many renters.
5. **Referral Programs:** Implement Resident referral programs that incentivize current Residents to refer friends or family, turning your existing Resident base into a marketing asset.

Leveraging Local Market Data for Targeted Advertising

Leveraging local market data effectively is a key component in amplifying the impact of your marketing efforts for property management. This data, rich with insights, provides an in-depth understanding of the specific demands, preferences, and trends prevalent in your area, enabling you to craft marketing strategies that are not just generic, but meticulously tailored to resonate with your local audience. By analyzing factors such as demographic profiles, local economic indicators, and competitor offerings, you gain the ability to align your marketing messages, promotions, and communication channels with the expectations and needs of potential residents in your community.

For instance, if market data reveals a growing number of young professionals moving into your area, you might focus your marketing on highlighting amenities like high-speed internet, modern fitness facilities, or proximity to urban hotspots. Alternatively, if data indicates a high demand for family-friendly living spaces, your marketing efforts could emphasize aspects like safety, nearby schools, and community events. This strategic use of local market data not only ensures that your marketing initiatives are more impactful and relevant but also enhances the effectiveness of your advertising spend. In doing so, it positions your property as an attractive option for prospective residents, leading to improved occupancy rates and ultimately, a stronger return on investment for your marketing activities.

Actionable Steps for Using Market Data:

1. **Gather Local Market Insights:** Regularly collect and analyze data on local rental trends, pricing, and Resident demographics. Tools like Zillow Research or local real estate market reports can be valuable resources.
2. **Segment Your Audience:** Based on your market research, segment your target audience and tailor your marketing messages to address the specific needs and preferences of each group.
3. **Adjust Strategies Based on Data:** Continuously refine your marketing strategies based on the insights gained from market data. Be adaptable to changes in market trends and Resident preferences.

How These Strategies Optimize Revenue:

- Targeted Marketing: By understanding and targeting your ideal Residents, you increase the likelihood of attracting and retaining renters, thus maintaining high occupancy rates.

- Market-Informed Pricing: Leveraging local market data helps in setting competitive rents, ensuring your pricing strategy is in line with market rates, which is crucial for maximizing revenue.
- Community Building: Engaging marketing efforts that focus on community building can lead to higher Resident satisfaction and retention, reducing turnover costs.

Conclusion

Effective marketing is an indispensable tool in the arsenal of property management. By employing a combination of creative marketing techniques and leveraging local market data, multifamily operators can minimize vacancies and optimize revenue. These strategies not only attract potential Residents but also contribute to building a vibrant and engaged Resident community.

Engaging Question for the Reader:

As you reflect on your current marketing strategies, ask yourself: How can you further tailor your marketing efforts to align with the specific needs of your target market, and what innovative techniques can you implement to make your property stand out in a crowded market?

In the next chapter, we delve into the importance of Resident retention programs, exploring strategies to enhance Resident satisfaction and loyalty, which are crucial for sustained revenue growth.

9
Developing Resident Retention Programs

*I*n property management, Resident retention is as crucial as attracting new renters. High Resident turnover can lead to increased costs and reduced revenue stability. This chapter focuses on developing effective Resident retention programs that build community and loyalty, outlining techniques to reduce turnover and maintain long-term Residents. By engaging with these strategies, multifamily operators can foster a supportive living environment while optimizing revenue.

Building Community and Loyalty Through Retention Strategies

Creating and nurturing a robust sense of community and a deep sense of belonging among residents is a cornerstone for successful property management, particularly when it comes to retention. When residents feel connected and valued within their living environment, they are naturally more inclined to renew their leases. This not only fosters a stable and vibrant community but also significantly diminishes the frequency and associated costs of resident turnover.

Enabling residents to feel at home goes beyond providing a physical space to live. It involves creating an atmosphere where they can form meaningful connections, feel a part of something larger, and genuinely enjoy their living experience. This sense of community can be cultivated through various initiatives and activities that encourage interaction, participation, and a shared sense of belonging.

For example, organizing regular community events, creating communal spaces that encourage casual interactions, and offering amenities that bring people together can all contribute to a stronger community bond. These could range from neighborhood gatherings, fitness classes, or cultural events to shared gardens and recreational areas.

Moreover, when residents are satisfied with their living environment, not only are they more likely to stay, but they also become advocates for the property, often referring friends and family. This word-of-mouth promotion is invaluable, as it comes from a place of genuine experience and satisfaction.

In essence, the effort to build and maintain a strong community among residents is a strategic investment. It leads to a harmonious living environment, reduces the churn rate of residents, and establishes the property as a desirable place to live. The resultant stability and positive reputation are fundamental for the long-term success and sustainability of a multifamily property.

Strategies for Building Community:

1. Regular Community Events: Organize events such as social gatherings, holiday parties, or educational workshops. These events encourage interactions among Residents, building a sense of community.
2. Feedback and Communication Channels: Establish open lines of communication. Regular surveys, suggestion boxes, and community meetings can provide Residents with a voice, making them feel valued and heard.
3. Responsive Management: Ensure that maintenance requests and concerns are addressed promptly and effectively. A responsive management team can significantly increase Resident satisfaction.

Techniques for Reducing Turnover and Maintaining Long-Term Residents

Minimizing resident turnover is a critical aspect of property management, as it not only leads to significant cost savings by reducing the expenses involved in attracting new residents but also plays a crucial role in fostering a stable and harmonious community atmosphere. High turnover rates often entail substantial costs, including marketing for new residents, preparing the unit for new occupants, and potential loss of rental income during vacancy periods. Moreover, a stable resident base contributes to a sense of continuity and community within the property, encouraging stronger relationships among residents and a deeper connection to the living space. This stability is often mirrored in the overall ambiance of the property, creating a more settled, cohesive, and engaged community. By implementing strategies that enhance resident satisfaction and engagement, multifamily operators can effectively reduce turnover rates, leading to a more vibrant and financially sound property.

Actionable Steps for Reducing Turnover:

1. Lease Renewal Incentives: Offer incentives for lease renewals, such as slight rent discounts, upgrades, or renewal bonuses.
2. Personalized Resident Experiences: Understand and acknowledge important events in Residents' lives. Simple gestures like birthday cards or welcome packages for new Residents can create a personalized experience.
3. Regular Property Upgrades: Continually invest in property improvements. Upgrading amenities, landscaping, and common areas can significantly enhance the living experience and encourage Residents to stay longer.

How These Strategies Optimize Revenue:

- Reduced Turnover Costs: By retaining Residents, properties can avoid costs associated with vacancy, advertising, and preparing units for new renters.
- Stable Revenue Stream: Long-term Residents provide a more stable and predictable revenue stream, essential for effective budgeting and financial planning.
- Positive Community Reputation: A strong community and high Resident satisfaction can lead to positive word-of-mouth referrals, reducing the need for extensive marketing efforts.

Conclusion

Developing robust Resident retention programs is a vital strategy in property management. These programs not only enhance the quality of life for Residents but also contribute to the financial health of the property. By focusing on community building, responsive management, and Resident appreciation, multifamily operators can create an environment where Residents are happy to stay for the long term.

Engaging Question for the Reader:

Reflect on your current Resident retention efforts: How can you further enhance the sense of community within your property, and what unique retention strategies could be implemented to make your Residents feel truly at home?

In the next chapter, we will explore the importance of conducting regular market analysis, highlighting its role in keeping your property competitive and aligned with current rental market trends.

10
Conducting Regular Market Analysis

*I*n the dynamic world of property management, staying informed about market trends is crucial for maintaining competitive pricing and services. This chapter delves into the importance of regular market analysis, outlining how it can help multifamily operators keep up with changes and optimize revenue. We will explore various tools and methods for ongoing market research, emphasizing how this knowledge can be leveraged to make informed decisions that enhance a property's profitability.

Keeping Up with Market Changes and Competitive Pricing

In the dynamic realm of property management, a keen understanding of and adaptability to market changes is crucial for crafting rental strategies that are both attractive to residents and financially beneficial for property owners. The ability to adjust rent prices in response to evolving market conditions is a balancing act; it requires a deep insight into the real estate market, an understanding of resident expectations, and a strategic approach to revenue management.

Setting rents that appeal to potential and current residents involves more than just following the market trends. It requires a comprehensive analysis of various factors, including demographic shifts, economic conditions, and local housing demands. For instance, a rise in demand for rental properties in a specific area due to an influx of new businesses or educational institutions calls for a strategic adjustment in rent prices, ensuring they align with the increased market value while remaining accessible to the target demographic.

Conversely, during periods of market downturns or increased competition, adapting rental prices to maintain occupancy becomes critical. This might mean offering competitive rates, flexible lease terms, or additional perks and amenities to retain existing residents and attract new ones. It's about creating a value proposition that resonates with the market's current state.

Moreover, understanding and adapting to market changes also involves anticipating future trends. This proactive approach allows multifamily operators to adjust their strategies ahead of time, positioning their properties advantageously in the market. Utilizing tools such as market analytics software, staying informed about local and national economic indicators, and engaging with real estate networks are all part of staying ahead of the curve.

In summary, understanding and adapting to market changes is a fundamental aspect of successful property management. It's about setting rents that not only attract and retain residents but also maximize revenue potential. This strategic approach ensures that properties remain competitive, desirable, and profitable in an ever-changing real estate landscape.

Strategies for Market Analysis:

1. **Regular Market Monitoring:** Keep a pulse on the local rental market by regularly monitoring trends in rent prices, Resident demographics, and demand fluctuations.
2. **Competitor Analysis:** Regularly review your competitors' pricing, amenities, and marketing strategies. This helps in understanding your position in the market and identifying areas for improvement.
3. **Economic and Demographic Trends:** Stay informed about broader economic and demographic trends that could impact the rental market, such as job market health, population shifts, or changes in housing demand.

Tools and Methods for Ongoing Market Research

In the dynamic world of multifamily property management, the power of effective market research cannot be overstated.

Embracing the right set of tools and methods for ongoing market analysis is pivotal in harvesting valuable insights, which are instrumental in strategically positioning your property in the ever-evolving market landscape. This approach isn't just about keeping pace with market trends; it's about staying ahead, making informed decisions, and tailoring your property to meet and exceed market expectations.

Key Tools and Methods:

1. **Real Estate Market Reports:** Utilize reports from real estate associations or market research firms to get a comprehensive overview of the rental market.
2. **Online Analytics Tools:** Leverage online tools like Zillow Research, CoStar, or local real estate websites to gather data on rental rates, occupancy rates, and other key market indicators.
3. **Resident Surveys:** Regularly survey your Residents to understand their satisfaction levels and what factors might influence their decision to renew their lease.

How Regular Market Analysis Optimizes Revenue:

- **Informed Pricing Decisions:** By staying informed about market rates and trends, you can adjust your pricing strategies to remain competitive and maximize revenue.
- **Anticipating Market Shifts:** Regular analysis allows you to anticipate market shifts and adjust your strategies

proactively, rather than reactively, positioning your property to capitalize on market opportunities.
- **Enhanced Resident Targeting:** Understanding current market demographics enables you to tailor your marketing and services to the needs of potential Residents, improving occupancy rates.

Conclusion

Conducting regular market analysis is a fundamental practice in effective property management. It equips multifamily operators with the knowledge to make informed decisions, ensuring their properties remain competitive and profitable in a changing market landscape.

Engaging Question for the Reader:

Consider how you currently monitor and analyze market trends: Are there additional tools or resources you could leverage to gain deeper insights? How might these insights influence your strategies to enhance occupancy rates and optimize revenue?

Summary: Key Strategies for Optimizing Multifamily Property Management

As we draw to a close on our enlightening journey through the Community yet vibrant world of multifamily property management, let's take a moment to reflect on the myriad of strategies and valuable insights we've unearthed along the way. This guide, meticulously crafted, serves as a powerful arsenal, equipping multifamily operators with the essential knowledge and tools to excel in every aspect of this dynamic field.

We began by delving into the intricacies of dynamic pricing models, uncovering the importance of flexible and responsive strategies in rent setting. Through this exploration, we discovered the power of advanced tools and software, learning to adeptly adjust rent prices in harmony with market demand and occupancy rates, thereby ensuring our properties maintain both competitiveness and profitability.

Our journey then navigated through the digital landscape, where we focused on creating a compelling online presence. We tapped into the vast potential of social media, digital marketing, and virtual tours, unlocking new ways to attract and connect with potential residents, thereby enhancing our properties' visibility in the digital world.

In the realm of value-added services, we explored how integrating amenities like on-demand laundry, high-speed internet, and pet-friendly options can significantly elevate resident satisfaction and open up new revenue streams. This exploration highlighted the importance of not just meeting but exceeding resident expectations to foster a thriving community.

The chapter on cost-effective unit upgrades shed light on the transformative impact of strategic improvements, such as modern appliances and smart home features. These enhancements not only elevate the appeal of units but also justify higher rental rates, thereby boosting the property's overall value.

We also turned our focus to energy efficiency, understanding how sustainable practices and appliances can significantly reduce operating costs and appeal to environmentally conscious residents, adding another layer of attractiveness to our properties.

The discussion on pet-friendly policies revealed the broadening appeal these initiatives bring, enriching our communities by catering to a diverse range of resident needs and preferences.

Key Strategies for Optimizing Multifamily Property Management

We then embarked on the creative journey of transforming unused spaces like rooftops and basements into lucrative amenities. This venture not only enhances the property's value but also boosts its community appeal, turning underutilized areas into vibrant hubs of activity.

In addressing strategies to minimize vacancies, we delved into effective techniques for maintaining high occupancy rates. We learned the importance of leveraging local market data for targeted advertising and ensuring our pricing strategies remain competitive and appealing to prospective residents.

One of our key focuses was developing resident retention programs. We discovered the immense value in building community bonds and fostering loyalty through personalized experiences and community events, strategies that are instrumental in reducing turnover and nurturing long-term resident relationships.

Finally, we emphasized the crucial role of regular market analysis. Keeping a pulse on market shifts and employing the right tools and methods for ongoing research is key to informed decision-making, ensuring we stay ahead in the ever-evolving property management landscape.

This comprehensive journey through multifamily property management has not only provided a wide array of strategies and practices essential for success but also offered a panoramic view of how these elements intertwine to create thriving communities. As we conclude this guide, we encourage you to weave these insights into your property management approach, aiming to build flourishing communities and achieve sustained success in your endeavors.

Engaging Question for the Reader:

Reflecting on the comprehensive journey through multifamily property management strategies, consider this: How can you integrate these diverse yet interconnected approaches - from dynamic pricing and online visibility to community building and market analysis - to not just enhance the operational efficiency and profitability of your property, but also to create a living environment that truly resonates with and enriches the lives of your Residents? How will these strategies shape the legacy and reputation of your property in the long term?

Each chapter of this book has been a lesson in property management and an invitation to innovate, adapt, and excel. The strategies discussed offer a roadmap to transforming your property management approach, focusing on maximizing revenue and creating vibrant, thriving communities where Residents feel valued and at home.

Remember, the journey in property management is continuous and ever-evolving. Stay curious, stay informed, and never hesitate to explore new avenues for improvement and growth. Here's to your success in building thriving, profitable, and community-focused properties!